For Matteo and Emilia
and all the kids in the world who are going through
a challenge and adventure of becoming big brothers and sisters.

Once upon a time there was a little boy named Matteo. He was living with his Mom and Dad in their small, beautiful house filled with love and lough.

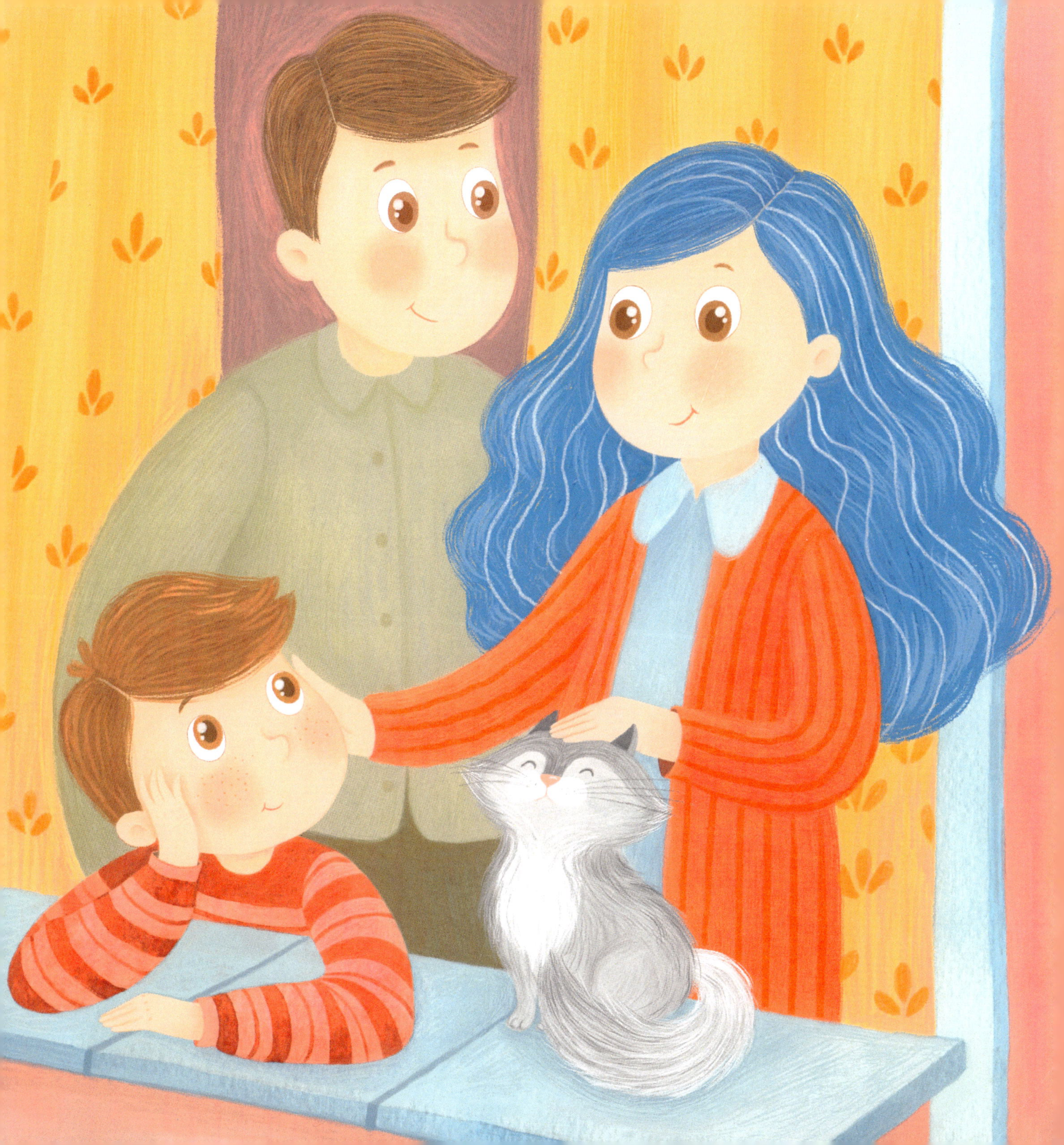

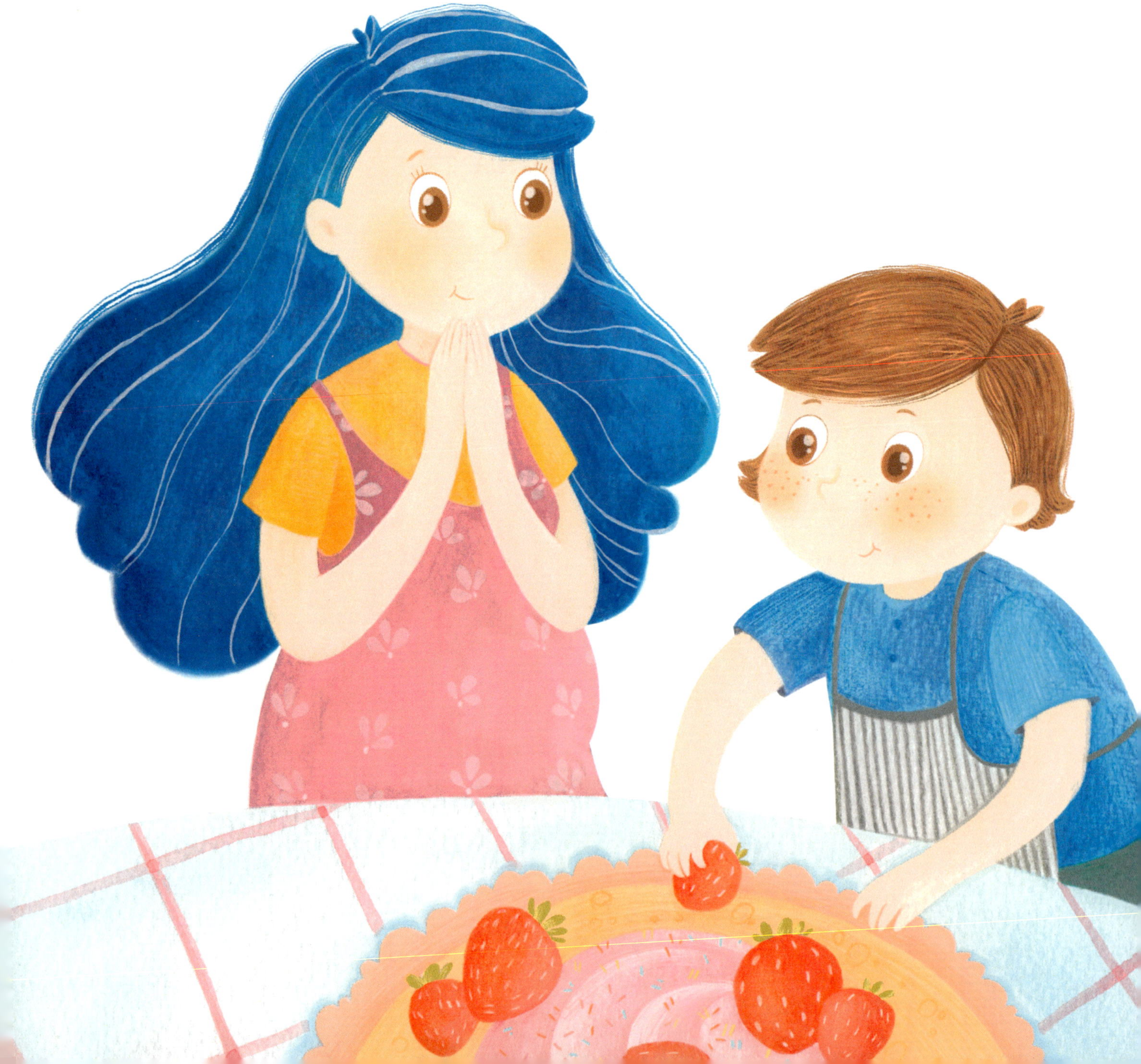

His Mom was the most beautiful and loving mother in the world. They were dancing and drawing together. She would cook him the most delicious pastas and fruit tarts. She knew many songs and games and every single evening they use to read a book or invent their own happy ending story. His Mom had the warmest arms and the sweetest kisses
in the entire universe.

Matteo's Dad was the most powerful and brave father in the in the whole wide world. He knew how to repair everything. He could lift him up to the sky even if he had grown big. He could lift even his mom, in that way that she seems to be light like a feather. That's how strong his father was. Matteo was delighted when his parents were laughing together. He was smiling and wishing to grow as big as his Dad so he could also take mom in his arms. Dad was teaching the boy how to play soccer and how to pick dandelions for his Mom. Matteo was feeling loved and precious in their small universe.

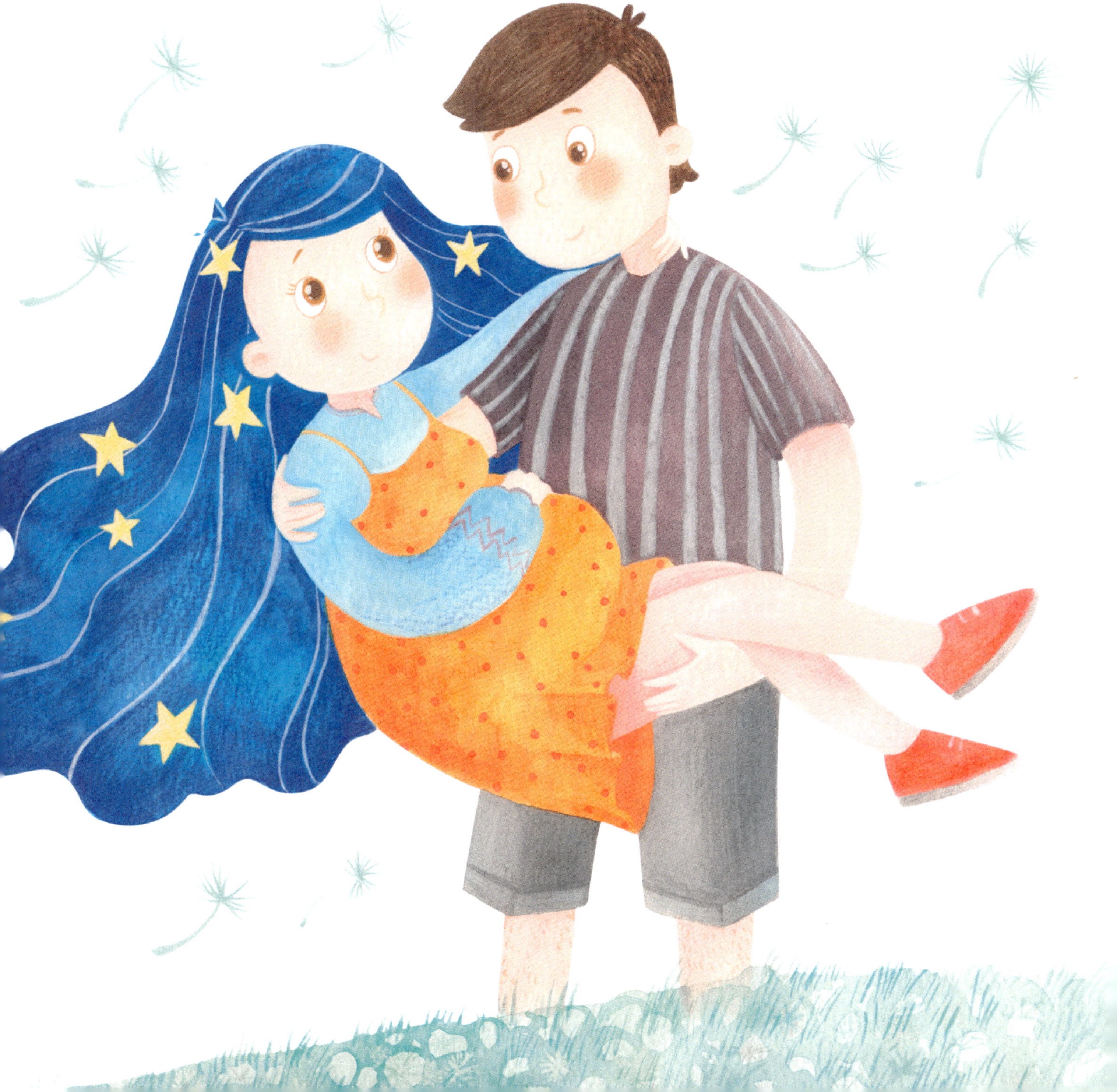

One-day Mom and Dad told Matteo that their family will grow bigger. They told him that they will have a baby that's growing up in Mommy's tummy. He would have a brother or a sister. But no doubts, he will be the big brother.

„Great!" thought Matteo and went back to his toys.

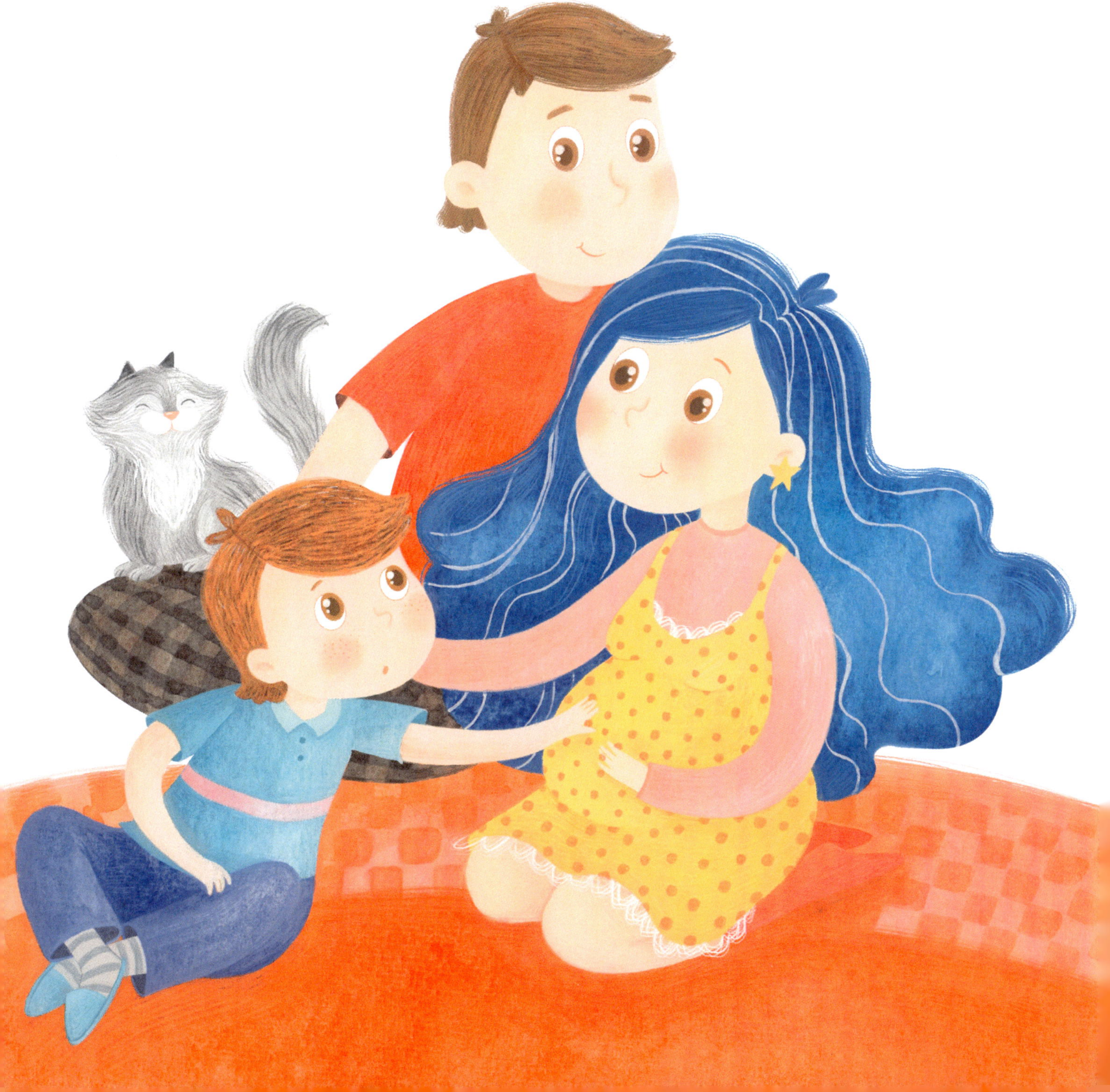

Mother's tommy gets bigger and bigger and his parents started to talk more and more about the baby. They talk about cribs, clothes, strollers and about „the big day".

„What does it means?" wondered Matteo. He was puzzled. How can a day be big or small? Aren't they all the same? Isn't a baby like a cat? All it needs is a plate for water and the another one for food. Why all this fuss?
he thought, confused.

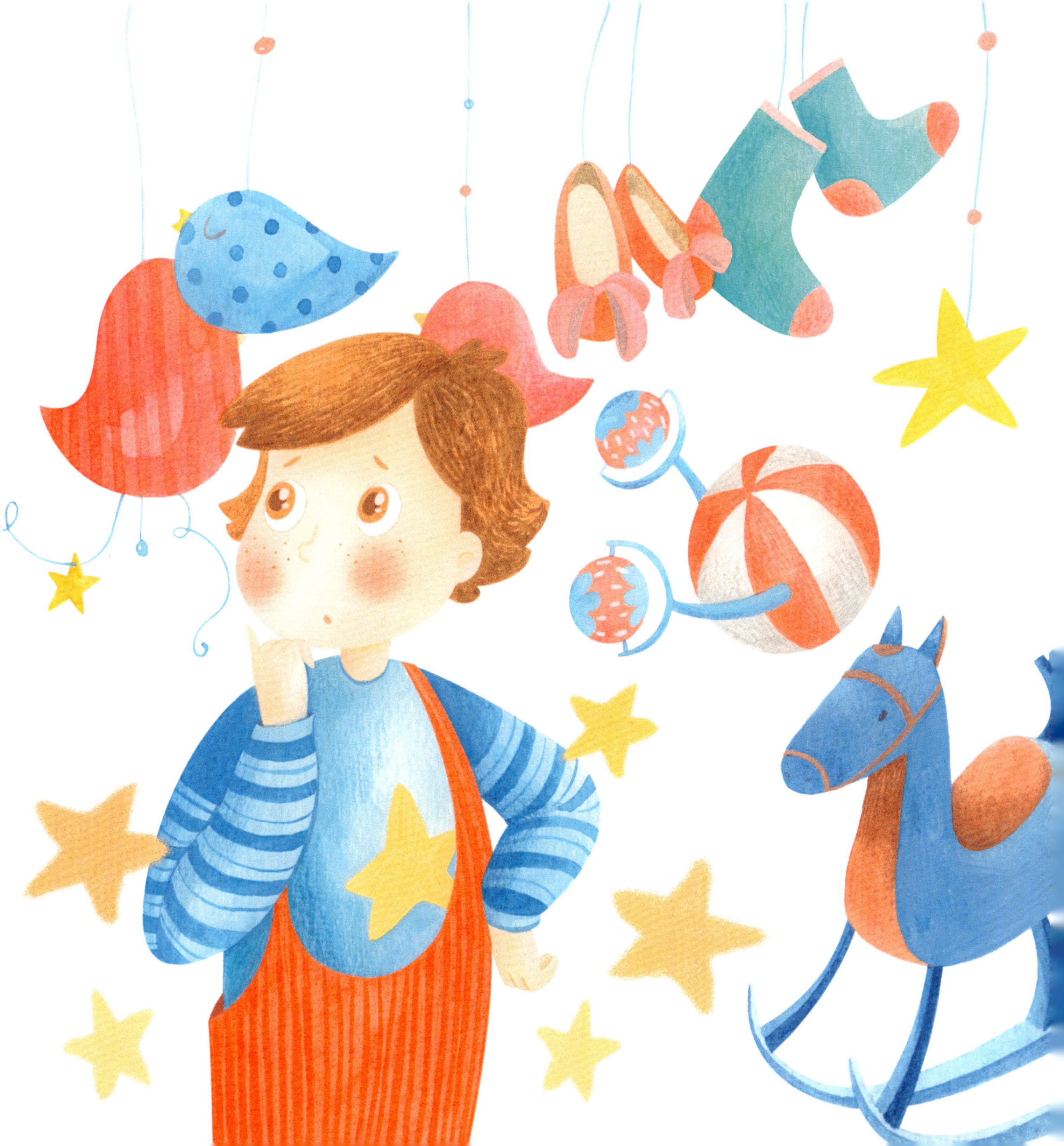

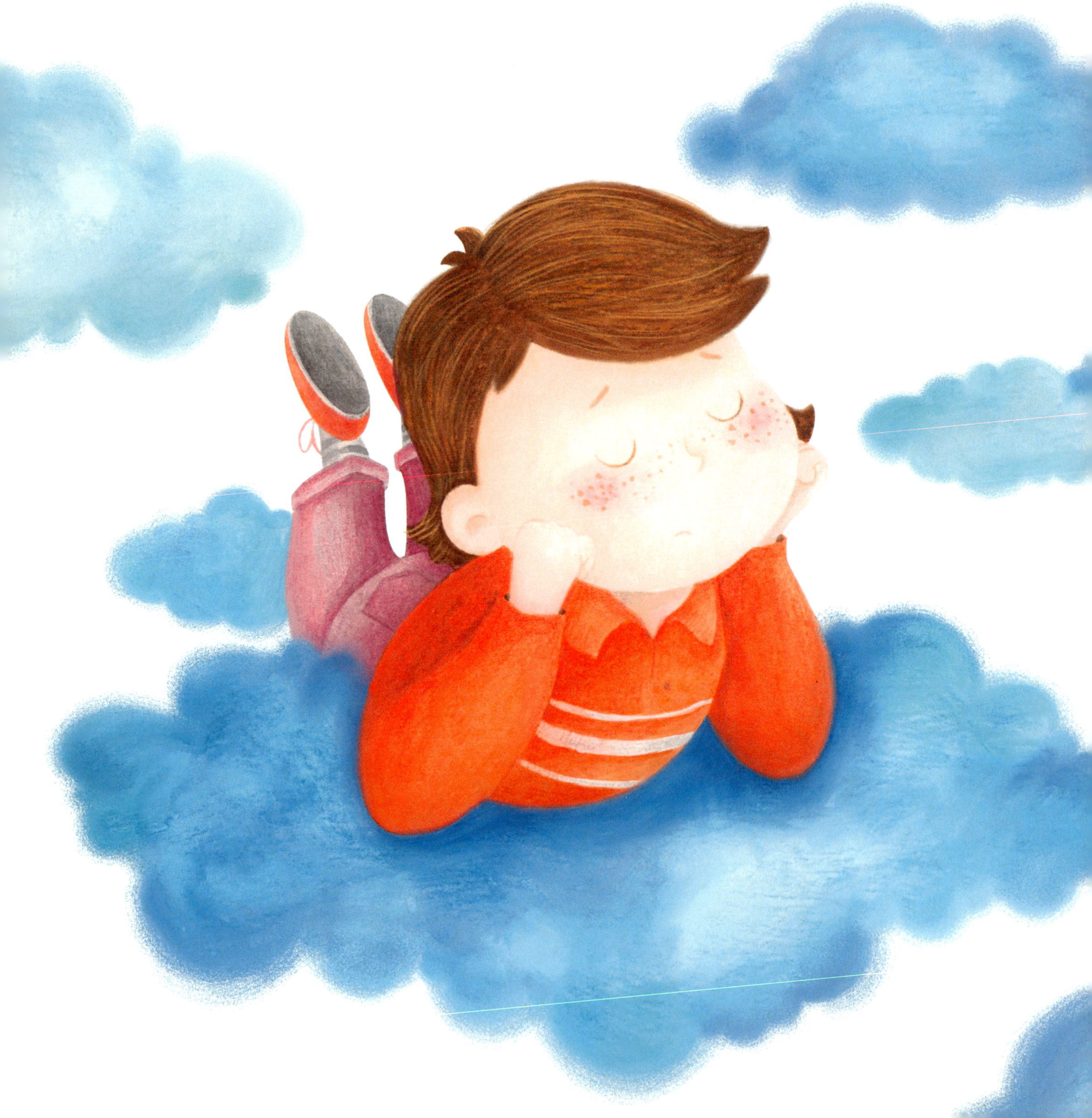

Mom said that very soon his little sister will come into the world. `Oh no! ` He hoped he will have a brother with whom he could play with his cars or play pirates.

—No! cried the boy. I don't want a sister! I want a brother! And there was silence in their house.

Mother and the little boy looked at each other. They both felt scared and confused. They got used to live like this, just the three of them. Now when the baby will come, how will it be like? Who will listen the bedtime story first? Who is going to take a bath first? Who will kiss Mommy first before going to bed? Matteo had so many questions in his little head, but he didn't know even how to tell his mother about all of them.

One day, when Dad came to pick up Matteo from school something strange was going on. He never saw his Dad like that. Dad's eyes were wet, but his face was bright and smiley. Matteo couldn't understand if he was sad or happy.

If he's happy, why does he have tears in his eyes? And if he's sad, why does he smile so wide? How it comes? Daddy quickly made his teachers smile as well. What happened?
Matteo didn't understand anything at all.

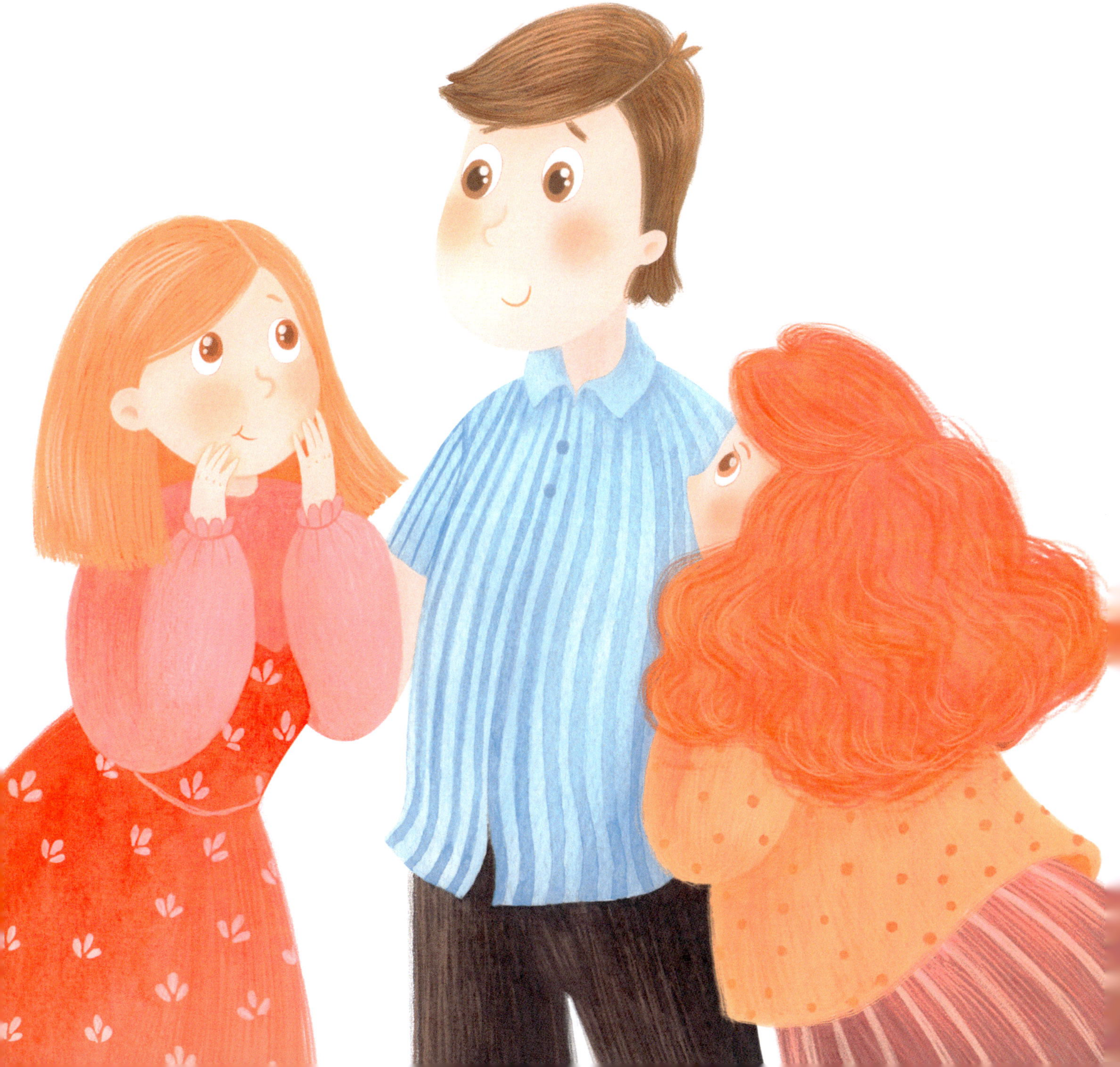

Dad came to Matteo, hugged him and said:

– You have become a big brother today. Your little sister was born. Today is her birthday.

Matteo didn't know what to say. He didn't have any idea how do babies that just came out of the mommy's tummy looks like. He got sad and few tears rolled down on his little cheeks. He couldn't smile as his Dad did.
He got scared.

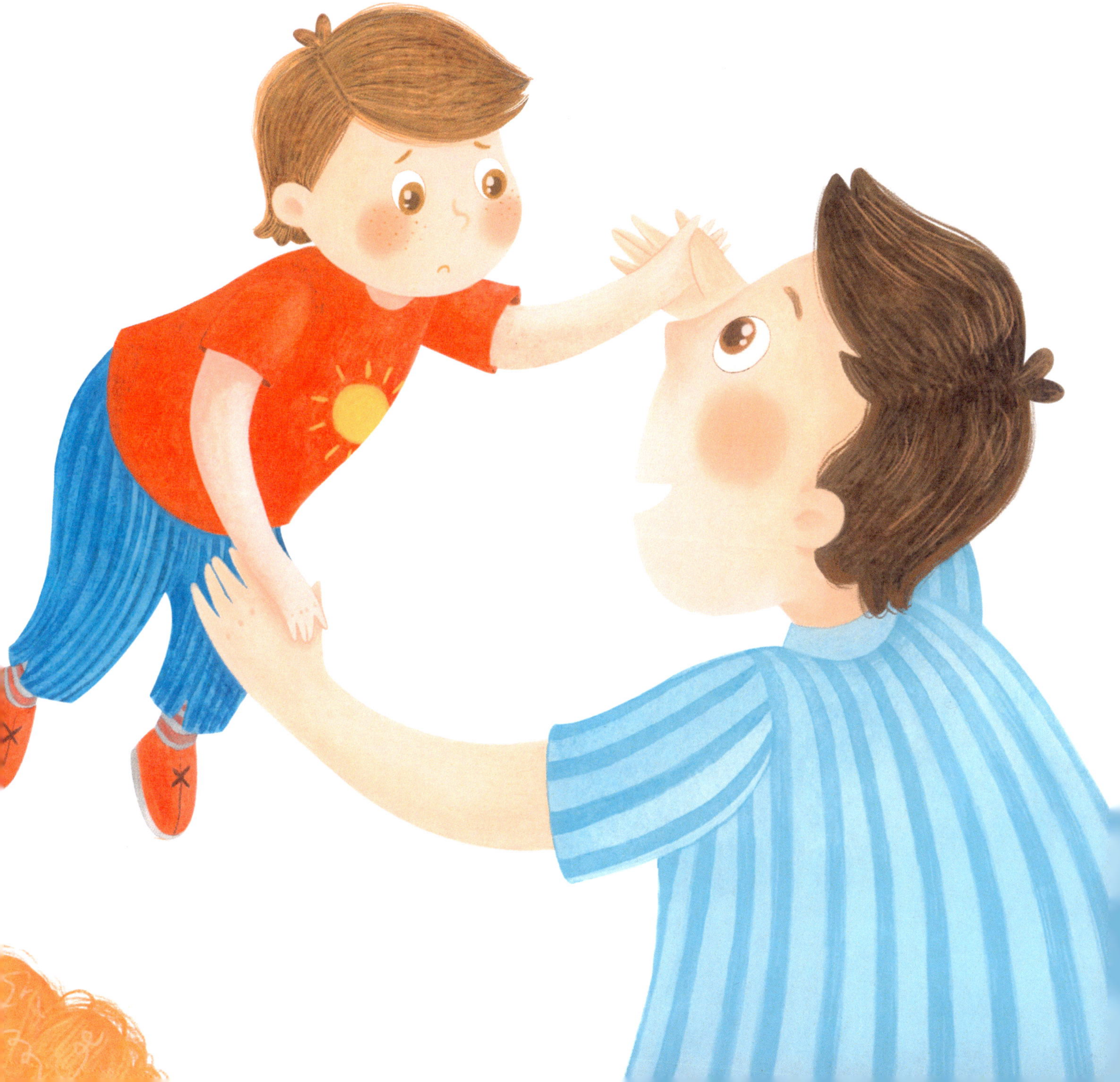

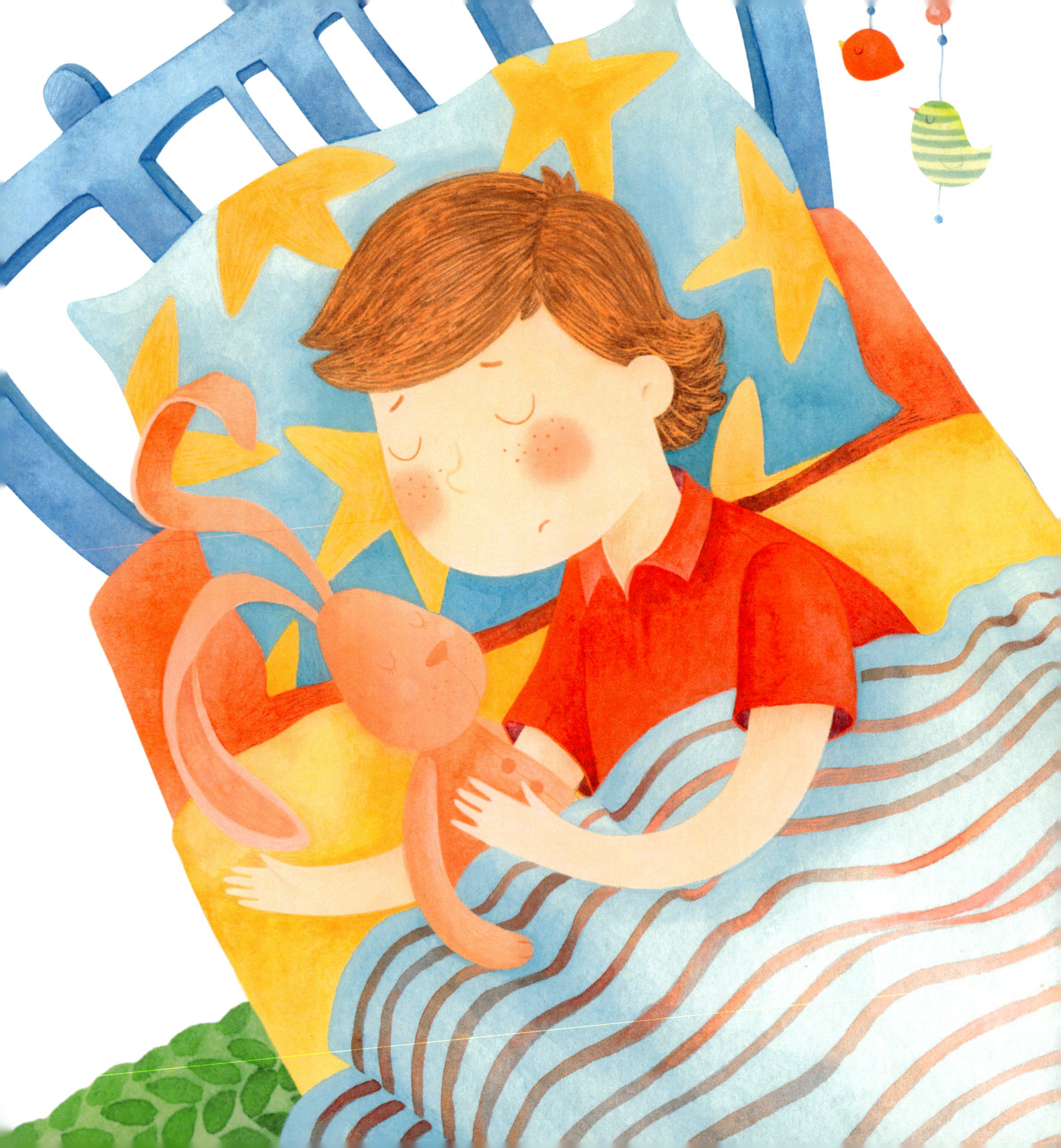

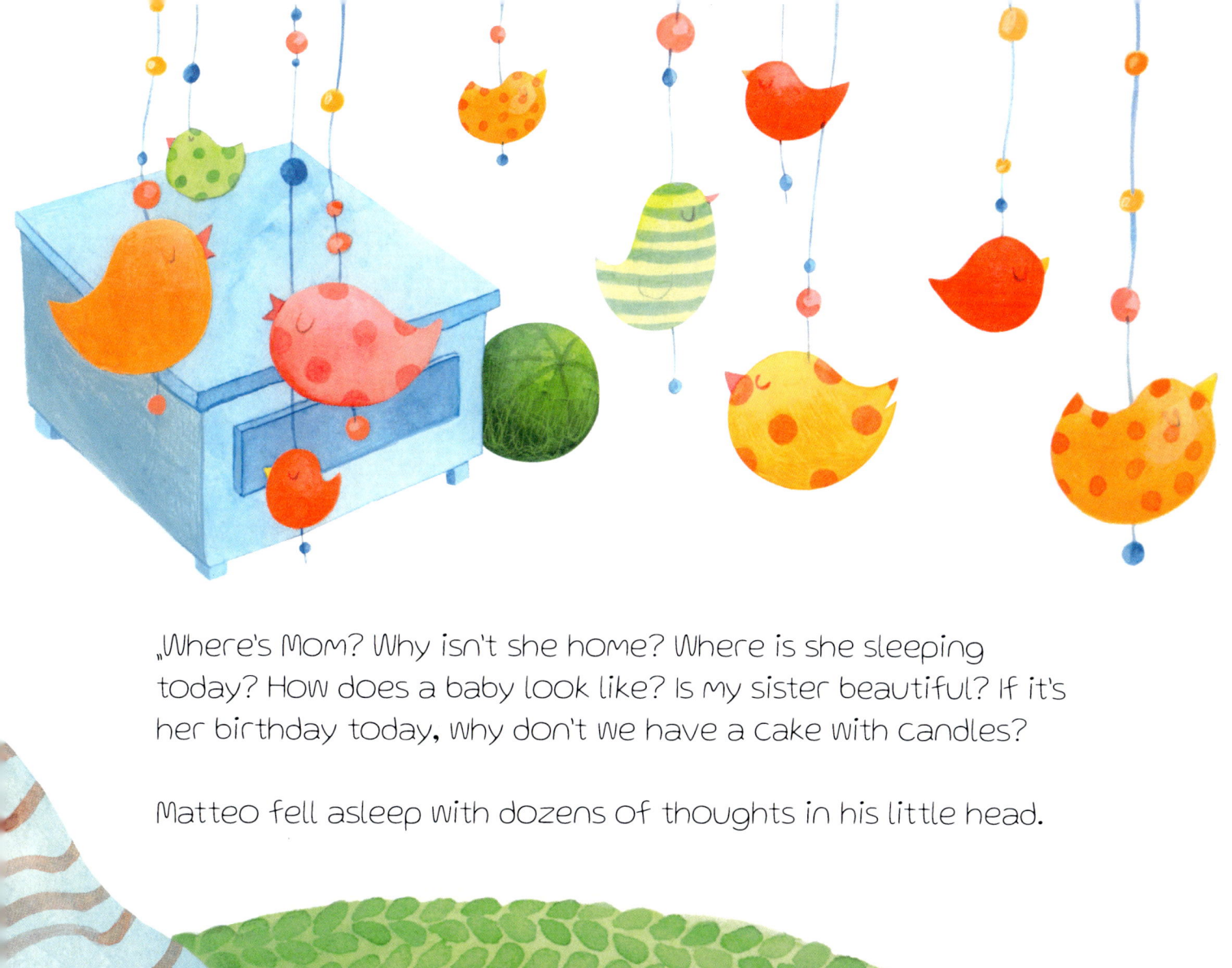

„Where's Mom? Why isn't she home? Where is she sleeping today? How does a baby look like? Is my sister beautiful? If it's her birthday today, why don't we have a cake with candles?

Matteo fell asleep with dozens of thoughts in his little head.

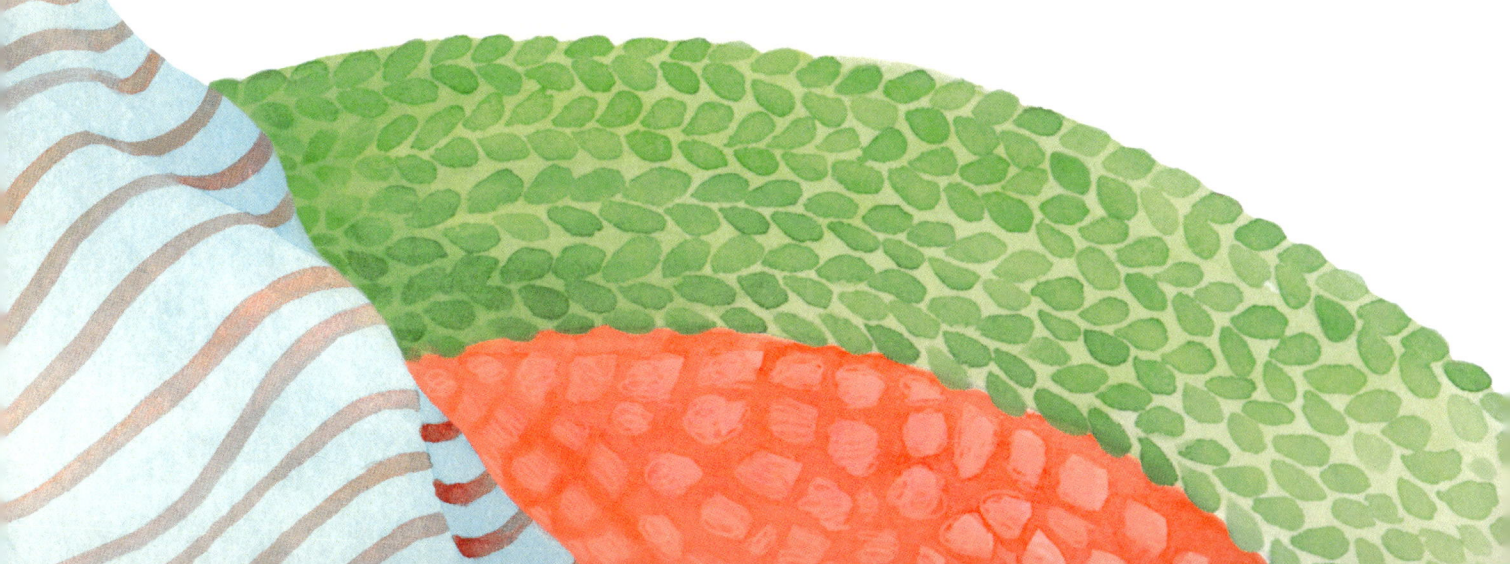

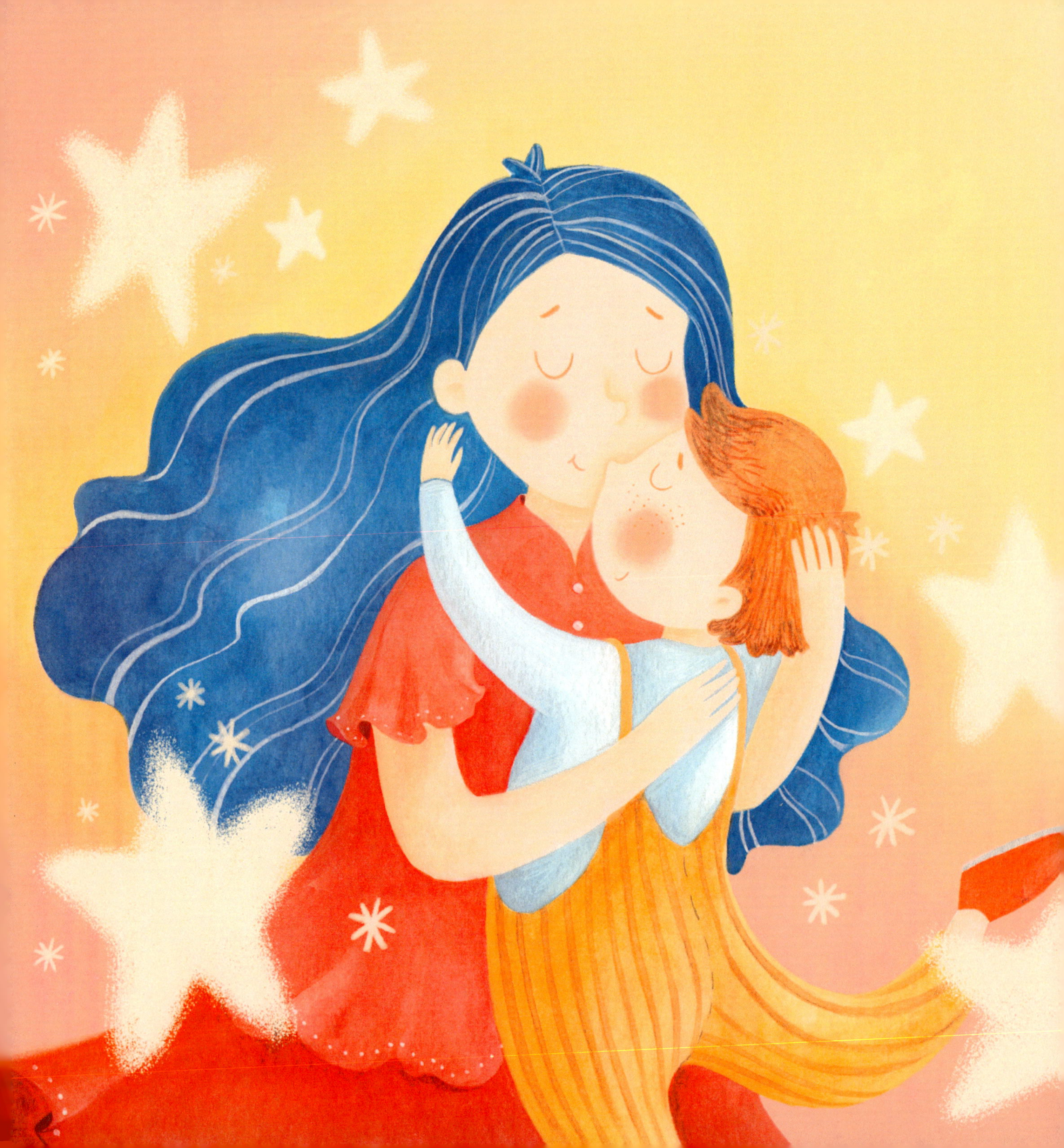

The next day he and Dad went to visit his Mom and sister.

„Mom!!!" he shouted and wrapped his hands around her neck as tight as he could, and then all his fears melted away.

„I love you, my dear! I've missed you so much!", said Mother and he felt like everything was back to normal.

Then Mom said:

- „Look, there is your little sister. Her name is Emy" pointing at a teeny-tiny baby looking like a doll. Matteo didn't say anything and didn't even understand what he was feeling. He was very curious how small his sister's hands were but didn't dare to touch them.

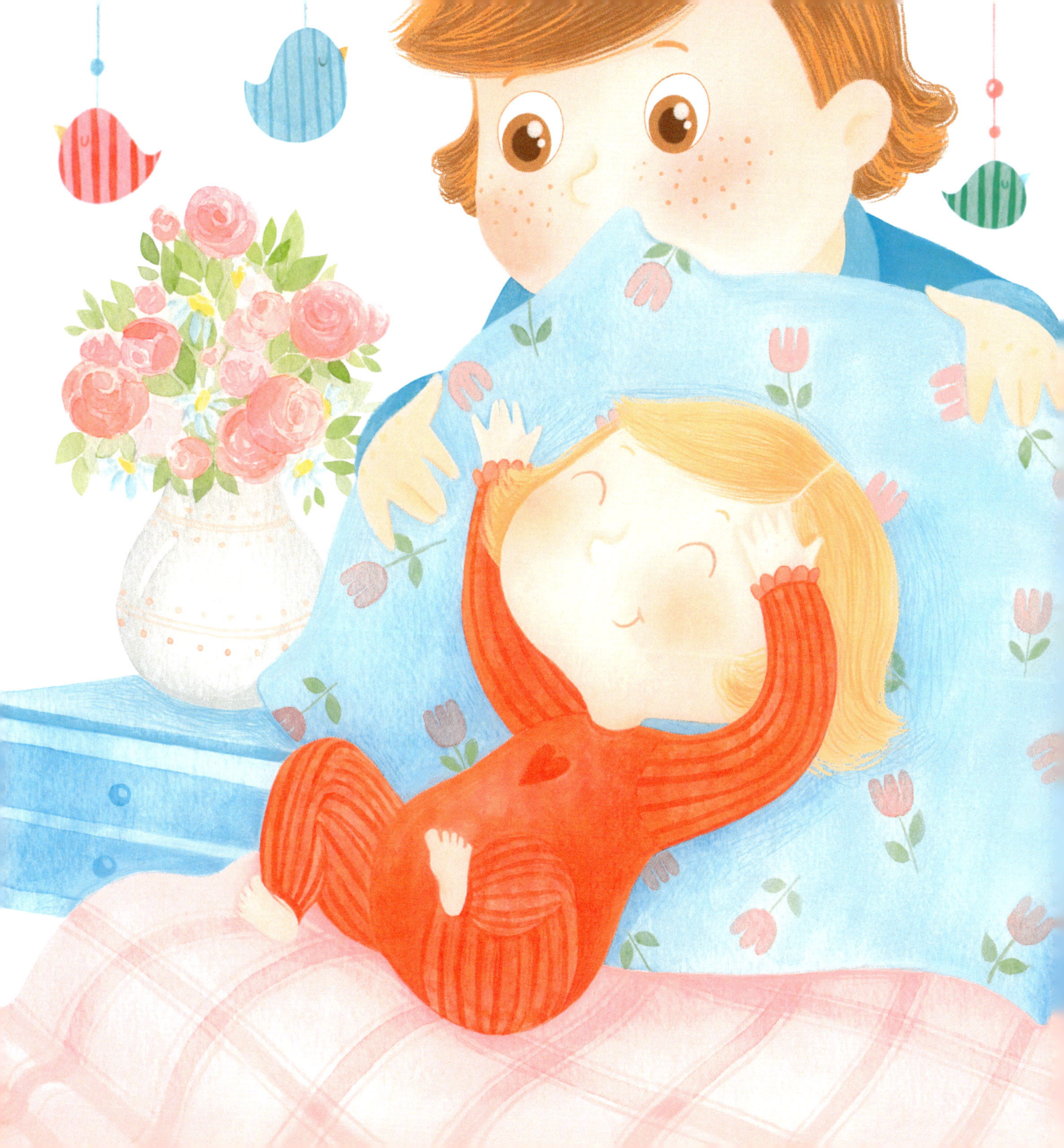

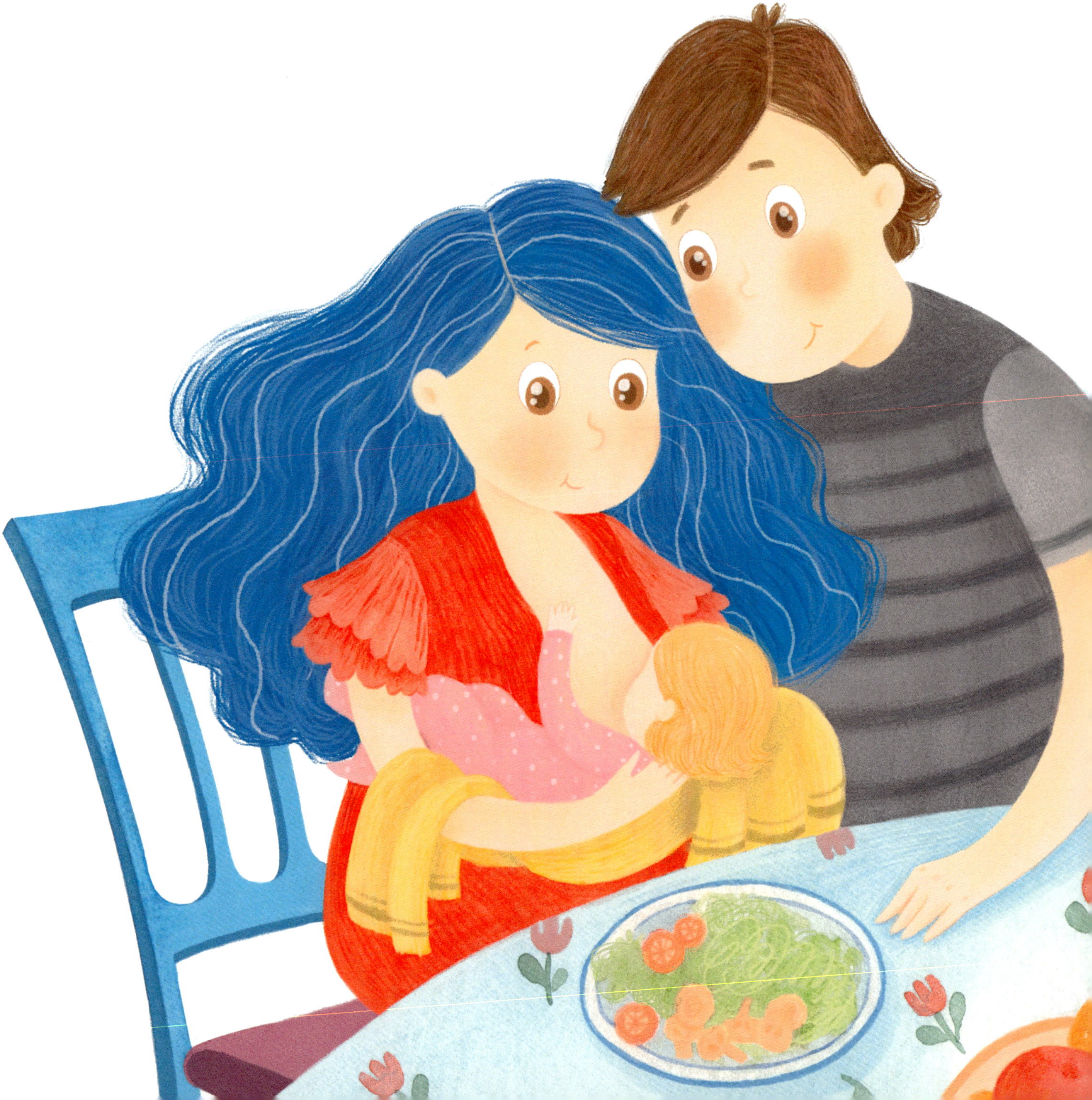

When his Mommy and the baby girl came home, they were all the time together like somebody stuck them to each other.

„Do babies have glue?" he thought. Mom was holding the baby in her arms all the time, all day long, even when she was cooking pasta for Matteo and when they were all sitting at the table. At least mom's pasta was just as good as before, and Matteo was happy to enjoyed it again.

That's how a few evenings have passed. Still, something strange was happening in Matteo's chest. It felt like a storm or a tornado of worry and fear that was disturbing him more and more.

„What if Mom and Dad don't love me anymore?" he thought scared, and began to cry with all the sadness that was hidden inside of him.

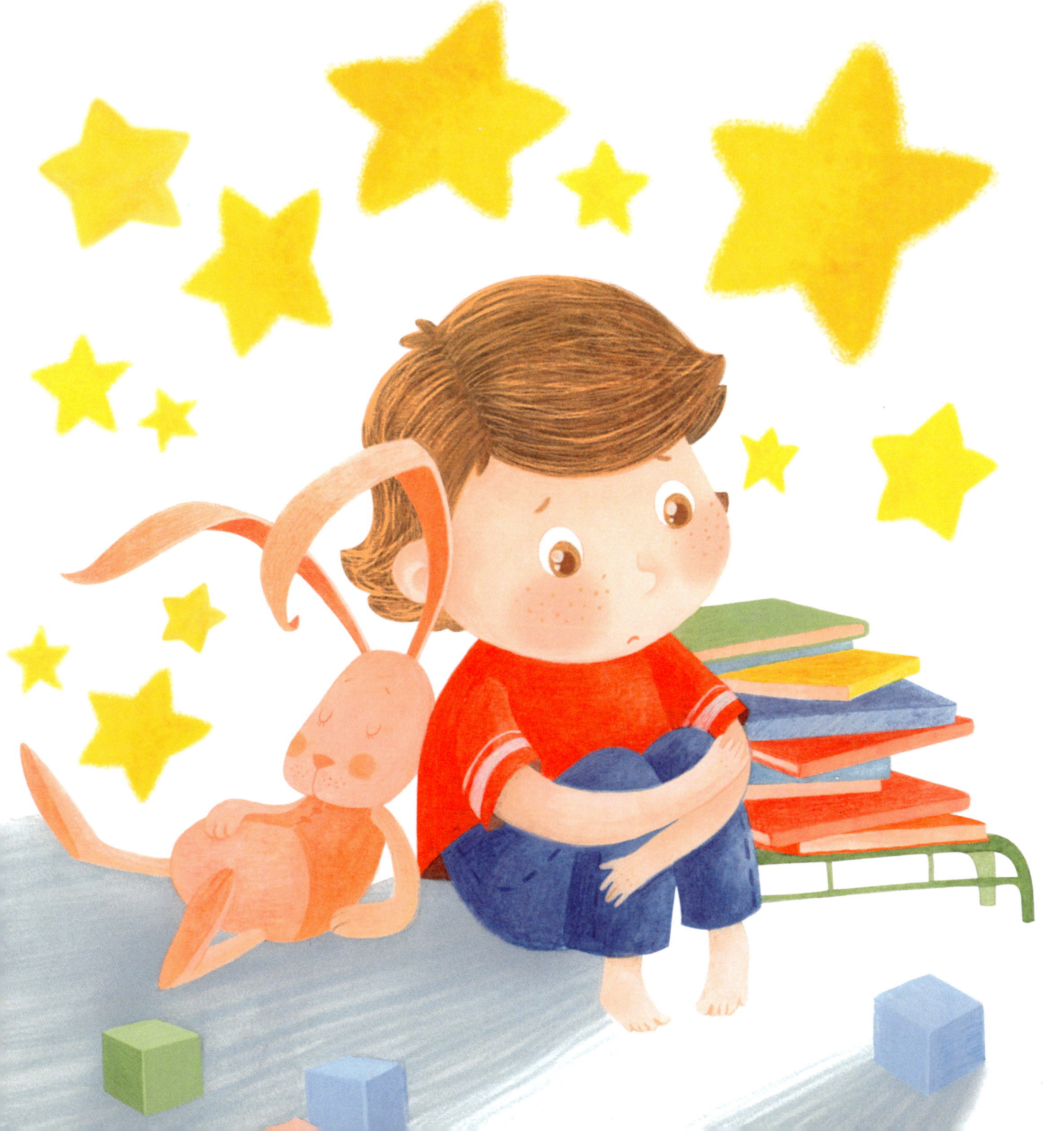

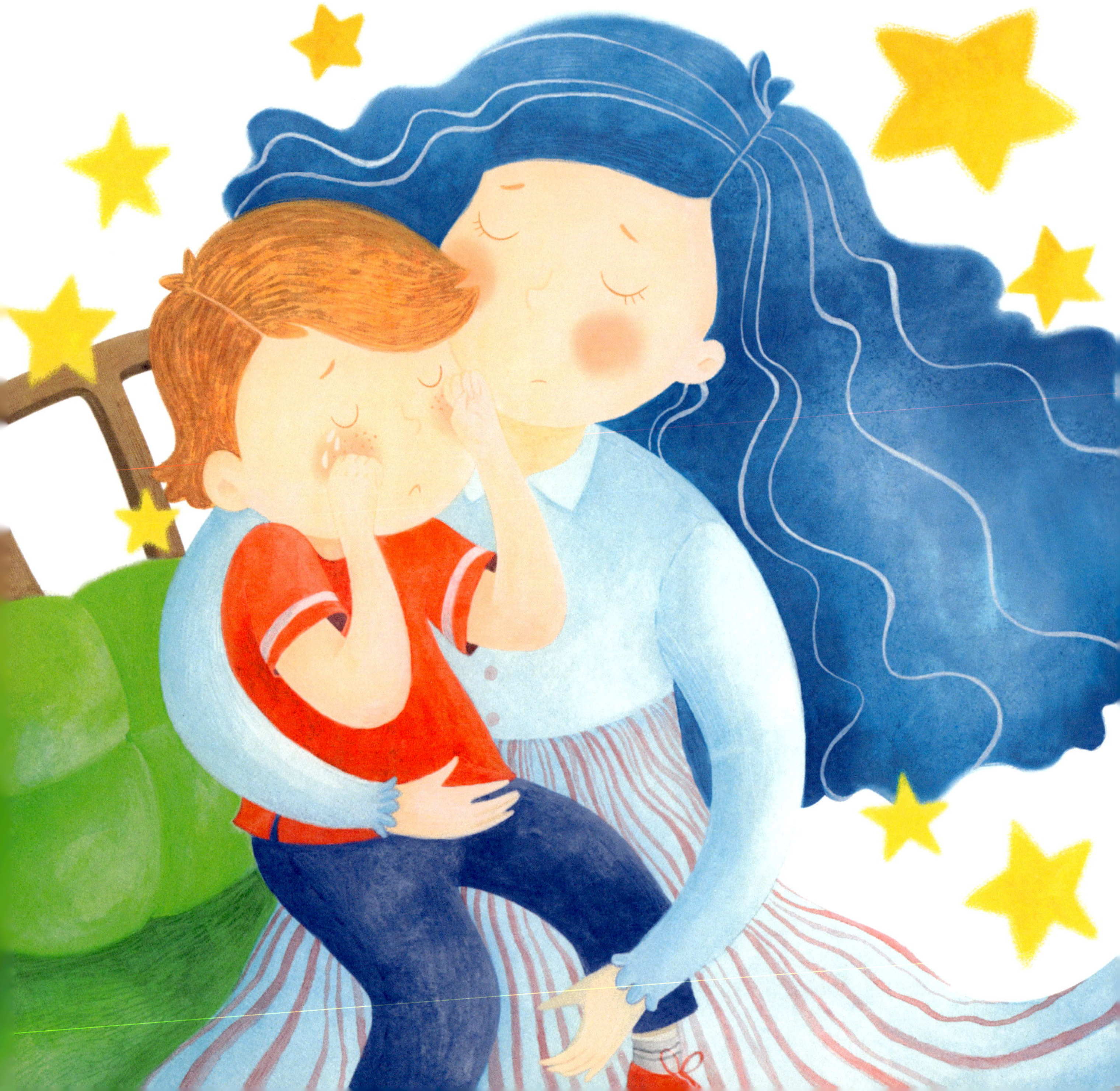

Mommy heard him and come quickly into his room. Holding his sister in her arms. Again!

- What happened? Are you okay? Asked Mom. Matteo began to cry even harder.
- Did you hurt yourself? Something hurts you? she asked again. She put the baby on Matteo's bed, hugged her little boy tightly and wiped away his tears.
- I don't want a sister! I want to be just me, you and Dad! Get her off my bed! It is mine! It is not hers!" he shouted angrily.

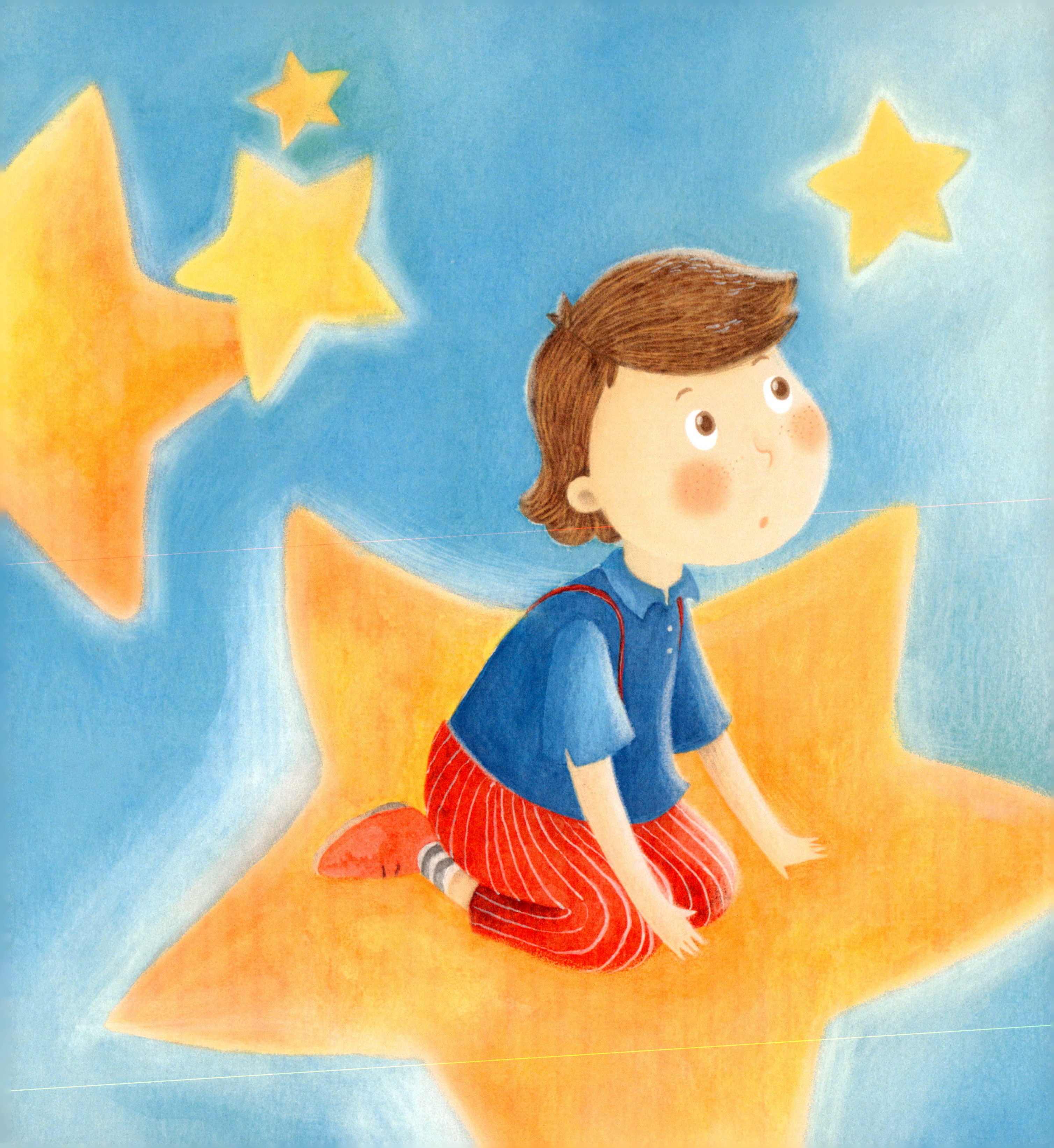

Mother's eyes filled with tears. She hugged him even more closely and warm while his little sister was sleeping peacefully on his bed, as if she didn't hear that it wasn't hers.

— Oh, my baby boy, I love you with all the love of all possible universes, said Mom.

Matteo knew that the universe is huge, enormous, infinite. How much his Mom loves him, if her love is as big as, not just one, but many universes? „Does she really love me so much? Even if she has another baby?" wondered the little boy.

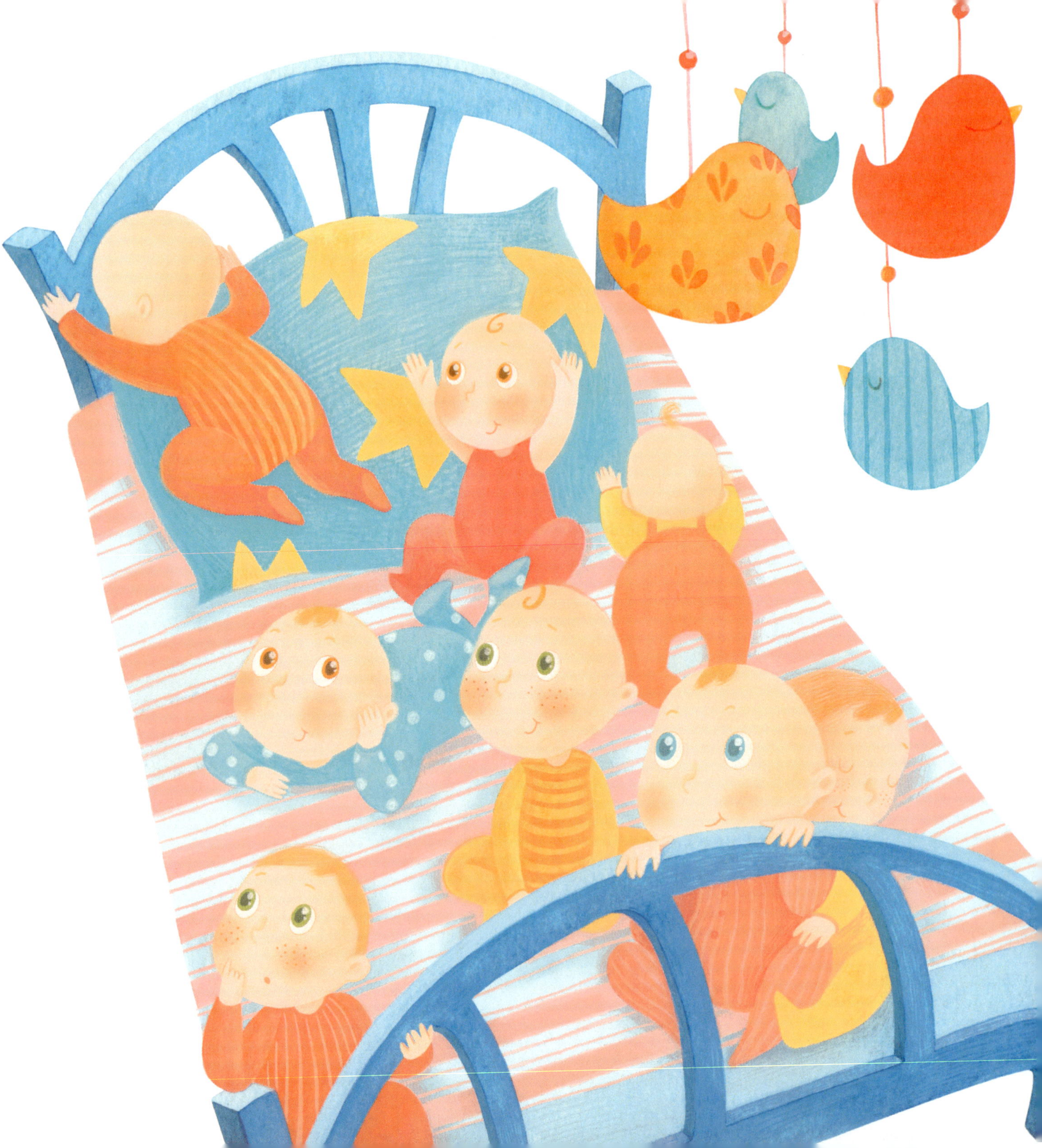

–	My love for you will never disappear anywhere, even if I have one more child. I will always love you, more and more each day. Even if I will have another ten or one hundred babies.

„One hundred babies?" thought Matteo and his eyes got big.

He looked at his bed and realized that if his Mom would want to put them all on it they certainly wouldn't fit. One hundred babies are a LOT. „Would one hundred babies fill up a universe? thought Matteo feeling amused, and a bright smile appeared on his face still striped with tears.

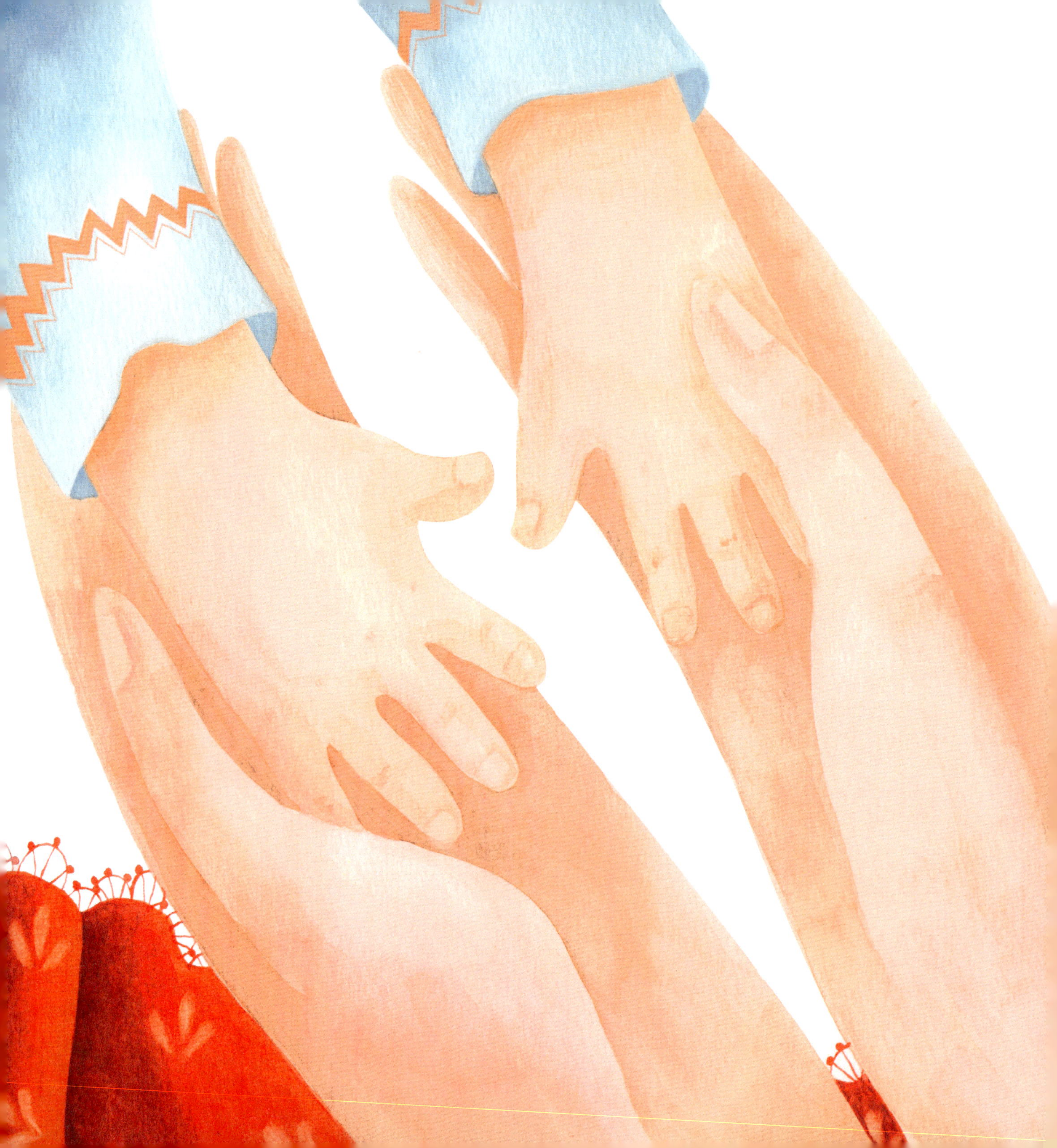

Mother took his little hands in her palms and said:

— My little love, you are the one who made us become Mom and Dad. You are the one who taught us and are still teaching us how to be parents. When you were born, Dad and I stayed up all night watching you. We were amazed by how wonderful and perfect you are. You brought so much happiness in our life that we were crying and laughing at the same time. You made us feel fulfilled.

„Oh! So Dad had that same strange face when I was born..." thought Matteo and smiled happily.

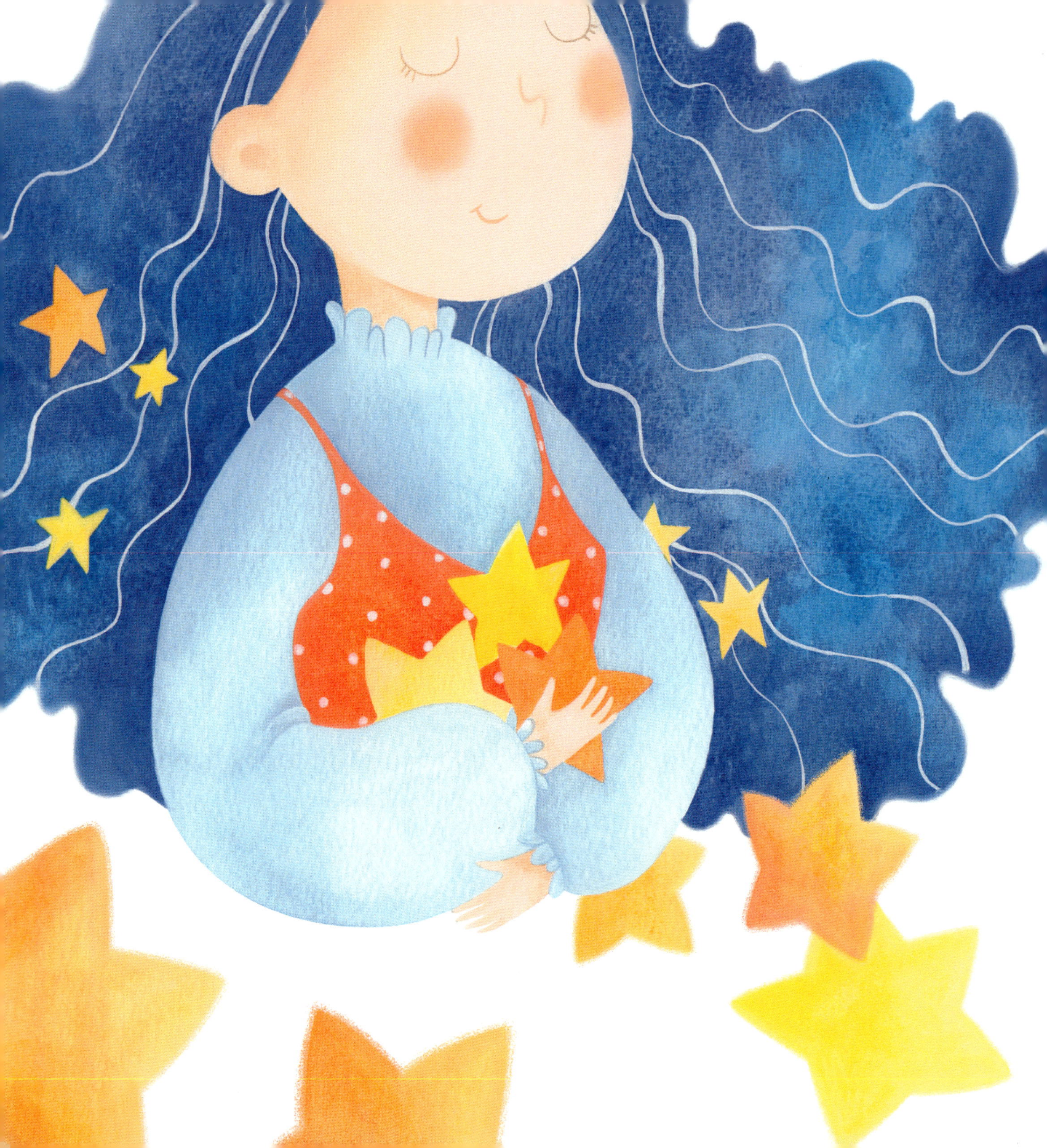

— My sunshine, my love isn't like a bread from which you break pieces and give to the others, you don't have to be scared that this bread won't reach everyone. My heart is as big as the sky and there it is enough place for many, many stars, but every little star is unique and enormously loved. There is enough love and place for all of you in my heart: for you, your father and your sister. There is place for grandma and grandpa and even for our cat. Love doesn't divide. It's growing and it becomes more and more, just like the dandelions in the park. No matter how many of them you pick, there will always be the others blooming.

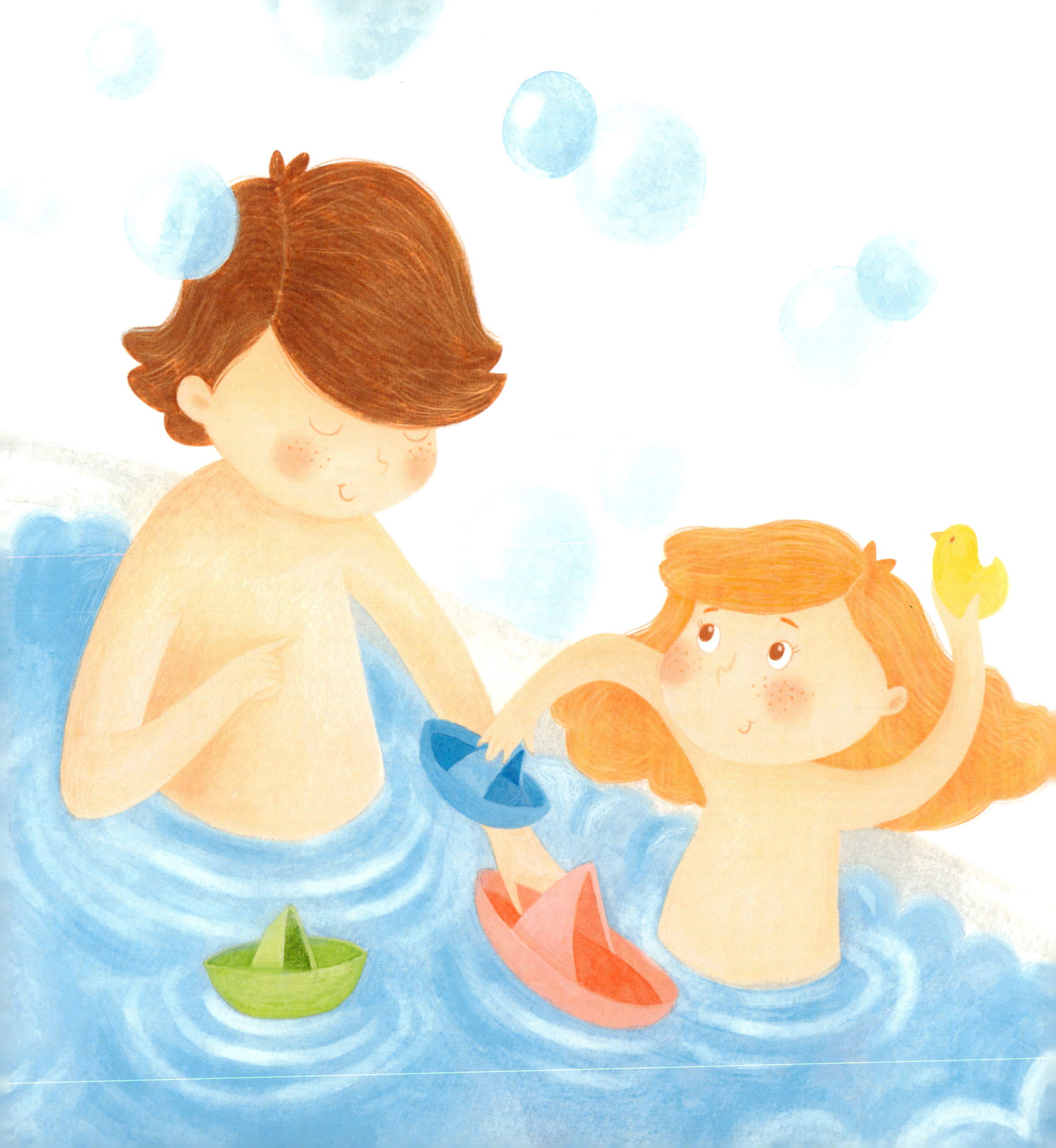

- Even if you will have one hundred babies? asked Matteo surprised.
- Even if I will have one hundred babies, laughed Mom wiping her tears.
- But how are we going to play now?
- We will learn how to play together, all four of us. We are four now and it will be more exciting.
- Who is going to take a bath first?
- You can choose every night if you want to be the first or the second one, and when your sister will be a little older you can take a bath together. You will show her how to play with the ships and cars in the tub.

Matteo smiled peacefully, then added:
- But who will get his bed time story first?
- We can read two stories together. One for you and one for your sister.

„Hm. Two stories sound better than just one" he thought.

The storm in Matteo's chest calmed down. He looked at Emy with his big eyes which are still wet, and smiled. Mother asked him if he wanted to touch her and he reached Emy's little hand with a pinch of shy and a big curiosity.

He held his sister little fist in his palm, it was warm and soft. It warmed his heart, too.

— Mommy, do you think my heart can be as big as the sky? he asked.

— I'm sure it is, Matteo. The more people we love; the more love we have in our hearts.

— You know what, Mommy? You can let Emy sleep in my bed and when she wakes up I will show her all my books about dinosaurs.

— Thank you, Matteo. I think she likes your bed if she sleeps so well, smiled Mom. She stepped out of the boy's room but was still keeping an eye on her sweethearts.

Matteo took his favorite bunny and put it next to his sister. He looked at her for a long time and slowly whispered

`She is beautiful. Just like Mommy`.

Then he sat down beside the car box and started playing with his toys.

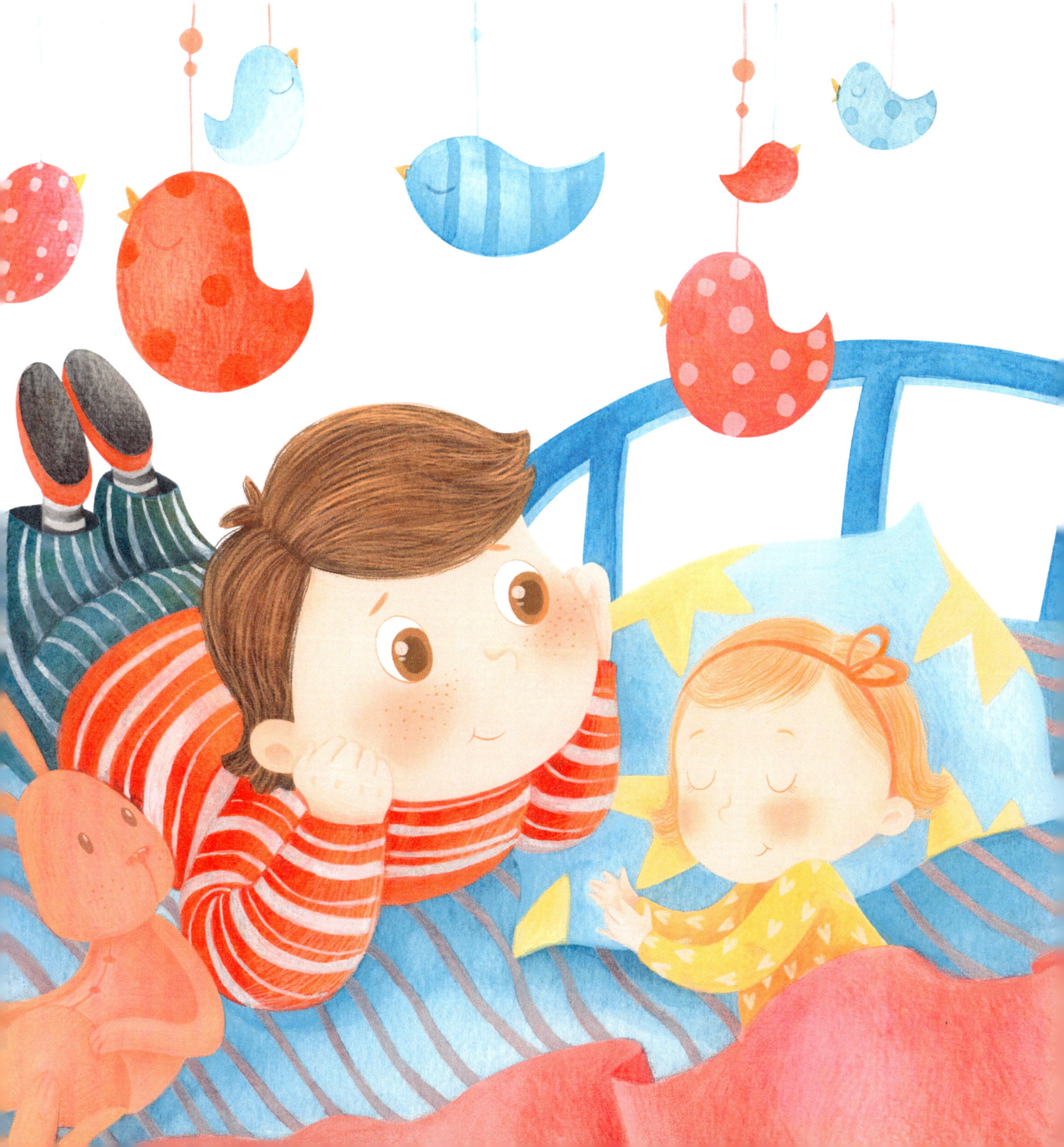

Author: Anastasia Popescu
Illustrator: Axenti Doina

Made in the USA
Las Vegas, NV
11 October 2022